SPOTTYSAURUS

SHARES

BREAKFAST

A BOOK ABOUT TRYING NEW FOODS
AND THE JOY OF SHARING

DINO MANOLI

Dedicated to Luca.

Thank you my number one son for believing in me

Spottysaurus was a dinosaur.

A fabulous blue dinosaur with a long blue neck, a huge blue belly and beautiful yellow eyes.

Spottysaurus was, in fact, blue all over, apart from one big bright pink spot on her back.

That big spot is why she was called Spottysaurus, but all her dinosaur friends called her Spot.

One day, Spot woke up in her huge dinosaur bed, yawned a big dinosaur yawn and stretched her long dinosaur neck.

She felt a rumbling and grumbling in her belly. It was so loud it shook her bed. Spot was hungry.

"Hmm. What shall I have to eat?" Spot asked herself.

"I'm so hungry I can't decide."

So, she left her cozy dinosaur cave and stomped slowly off through the forest
to see if a walk would help her think of what to have for breakfast.

After a little while, Spot bumped into her friend Spike, the Stegosaurus.

"Hello, Spot," Spike said cheerfully, "What are you up to?"

Spot stopped her stomping, smiled at Spike and said "I'm having a walk to help
me decide what I should have for breakfast."

"What are you eating?" asked Spot.

"I'm having some cheese," said Spike.

"Yummy, yummy, yummy, all that tasty deliciousness in my belly," said Spike, licking his lips.

"I love it!"

"Hmm, I don't think I've ever eaten cheese for breakfast," said Spot. "Maybe I should try it. Trying new things is exciting. Thank you for a great idea!"

And off she stomped, wondering if she would like to eat some cheese for breakfast and where she could find some.

After a while, Spot bumped into her friend Toni, the T-Rex.

"Hello Spot" Toni roared with glee to her friend, "What are you up to?"

Spot stopped her stomping, smiled at Toni and said, "I'm having a walk to help me decide what I should have for breakfast."

"What are you eating?" asked Spot.

"I'm having some meat," said Toni.

"Yummy, yummy, yummy, all that juicy deliciousness in my belly," said Toni, licking her lips.

"I love it!"

"Hmm, I don't think I've ever eaten meat for breakfast," said Spot.

"Maybe I should try it. Trying new things is exciting. Thank you for a great idea!" And off she stomped, wondering if she would like to eat some meat for breakfast and where she could find some.

After a while, Spot bumped into her friend Barry, the Brachiosaurus.

"Hello, Spot," said Barry in a deep booming voice. "What are you up to?"

Spot stopped her stomping, smiled at Barry and said, "I'm having a walk to help me decide what I should have for breakfast."

"What are you eating?" asked Spot.

"I'm having some Lettuce," said Barry.

"Yummy, yummy, yummy, all that crunchy deliciousness in my belly", replied Barry, licking his lips.

"I love it!"

"Hmm, I don't think I've ever eaten lettuce for breakfast," said Spot. "Maybe I should try it. Trying new things is exciting. Thank you for a great idea!"

And off she stomped, wondering if she would like to eat some lettuce for breakfast and where she could find some.

After some more slow stomping, Spot sat down by a river and had a little drink.

She was still not sure what to eat, but she knew she was very hungry.

As she sat there thinking, she felt a rumbling.

"Oh dear, there goes my belly again", she said to herself, "And this time, it's so loud it's even making the ground shake."

But, to her surprise, it wasn't her belly making the ground shake. As she looked around, she saw Spike, Toni and Barry all walking and stomping towards her… and they were all bringing food to Spot.

Spike was rolling a wheel of cheese along with his nose.

Toni was carrying a huge piece of meat in her tiny arms.

Barry had a big ball of Lettuce balanced on his back.

"We wanted to share our breakfast with you!" they all roared happily.

"I've brought some tasty cheese to share," said Spike

"I've brought some juicy meat to share," said Toni

"I've brought some crunchy lettuce to share," said Barry

Spot smiled a huge happy smile and thundered out a "Thank you, my fabulous friends."

And with that, they all sat down in a circle and shared their food.

"This is the best breakfast ever," said Spot and she carried on crunching, munching and chomping until her tummy stopped rumbling.

Story Activity Time

Which Dinosaurs liked which food ?

Trace a line with your finger to connect the Dinosaur with their favourite food.

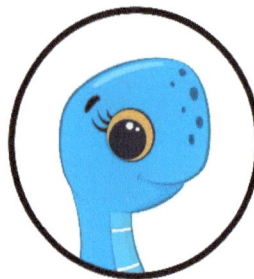

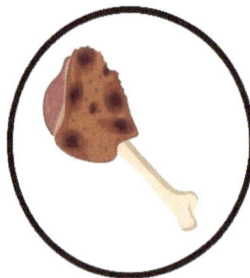

Story Activity Time

Describing Dinosaur food. Point to the Dinosaur food which is... "Crunchy", "Juicy", "Tasty", "Your favourite"

Story Activity Time

Which Dinosaur tried new foods with her friends?

www.ingramcontent.com/pod-product-compliance
Lightning Source LLC
Chambersburg PA
CBHW041241020426
42333CB00002B/45